COLOR

COLOR

HERBERT E. MARTINI

THIRD EDITION

BRIDGMAN PUBLISHERS

PELHAM · NEW YORK

NOTE

The following color plates appear as a special insert between pages 32 and 33 of this book:

PRIMARY COLORS

SECONDARY COLORS

COMPLEMENTS

VALUES

Acknowledgment and thanks are due Mr. Archie Griffin for his valuable assistance in supervising the production of these plates.

PREFACE

The value of a book of this scope lies in the practical experience it reflects, in that this shortens the experimental work of the artist or student by directing it along proper channels. It is, however, of prime importance that there be a serious effort on the part of the reader to carry out the most obvious work as described—for a description without actual experience is of no value. As an analogy —thousands of chemistry students actually do chemical experiments of the simplest nature even though they are thoroughly familiar with the process and results from descriptions. Theory must be backed up with practice.

CONTENTS

CHAPTER I

TOOLS OF THE ARTIST

OIL PAINTING

The equipment for painting in oil colors should consist of a wooden palette of a convenient size and shape which balances with least strain on the hand and thumb of the hand holding it. The new palette should be rubbed with a rag moistened with linseed oil and then allowed to dry about a week. This fills up the pores of the wood and gives a workable surface. Then you need a flexible palette knife which is used for mixing larger quantities of tints or for cleaning the palette when the day's work is done. The knife is also useful for removing the color from the canvas of those parts which are to be changed in either drawing or color. If the subject and your technic demand it, the palette knife can be used instead of the brush for applying the paint to the canvas. An oil cup with a clip to fasten it to the palette is necessary. Some artists prefer two cups—one with the painting medium and the other filled with turpentine to clean the brushes while working. The brushes should consist of an assortment of flat and round bristle brushes and a few hair brushes. The bristle brushes when new usually have their hairs moistened with glue

[11]

to keep them in shape in the dealer's case, so rinse these in lukewarm water before using them the first time. After the day's work is completed, clean all your tools carefully. Remove all the paint from the palette and then clean it off with a rag wetted with kerosene. Rinse your brushes with kerosene, then wash them with a mild soap and warm water. After they are rinsed squeeze out the water, shaping the hairs of the brush to their intended point and lay them aside to dry. The assortment of pigments can be chosen from the list in the next chapter or for definite types of work the suggestions found there should determine your choice.

WATER COLOR PAINTING

For studio work a flat porcelain palette and a porcelain slab with indentations are most desirable, whereas for sketching outdoors a paint box with a double cover, the one equivalent to the flat palette, the other to the indented dish, is the most convenient. Two glasses for water should be used in the studio. One should only be used for rinsing out brushes before proceeding with another tint. The water in the other should be kept as clear as possible and should be the supply to use for thinning and mixing your colors. When working outdoors you will find the water containers made of nickeled tin handy; especially those in which the covering of one end forms the water cup with clip to attach it to your color box. The brushes in this technic are usually round sable, large brushes being used for the washes; the smaller ones for details. For the student, camel's hair brushes give admirable service. It is advisable to wash the brushes occasionally with lukewarm water and a mild soap. Dry and shape brush as previously directed.

TEMPERA PAINTING

Although this medium has primarily been used for poster and design work in this country many artists are finding the attractiveness of its brilliant colors interesting in both still-life, landscape and figure rendition. It has the easy working quality of water color but can be handled in opaque fashion similar to oil. The palette for this medium may be white enameled wood, tin, or aluminum. The equipment for water, which is the painting medium, may be the same as for water color. For outdoor work the same type of box as for water color is suitable, or an oil color thumb box can be used, the palette of which has been enameled white with a good nitro-cellulose lacquer. The brushes can be either sable or bristle depending on the technic you aim for. As true tempera contains oils and gums which become water insoluble,

[13]

it is necessary to wash the brushes with soap and water before putting them away. Do not forget to squeeze out the water with the fingers and shape each brush. It adds to its life.

CHAPTER II

PIGMENTS

From earliest times color has been of importance to every cultural development. About 2500 B. C. but six simple pigments were used but our pigments today are known by several hundred names and the artist as well as the beginner sometimes finds himself bewildered when he studies the dealers' color lists.

The artist of years ago had an intimate knowledge of his pigments because he was compelled to prepare them himself. It is this knowledge of their characteristics and application which has preserved many of the old masters' works rather than the quality of the material they used. Within the last hundred years science has given us pigments of absolute permanency and greater beauty than were known to the old masters. Unfortunately many colors were also produced without any intention that they be used by the artist. They are very alluring in their nuance and brilliance but very fugitive.

In the color list following we will give the composition and character of each pigment and name the vehicle in which it is most generally used. We will point out which colors are compatible; and which are not. We will also asterisk those which

[15]

should form the basis of the simplified palette. A recent survey undertaken by the writer has shown that about 12 to 18 colors are generally used by over 80% of the best artists of today.

Note:—The letters O. W. T. at the end of the description of a pigment indicate the vehicle in which that pigment is usually ground i. e., O, for oil; W, for water and T, for tempera.

WHITES

FLAKE WHITE, basic lead carbonate, also known as Cremnitz and Silver White. Known by the Romans. It is a heavy color with great body. It is affected by sulphur gases and sulphur colors (Cadmiums, Vermilions, Ultramarines). It is not compatible with the copper color, Emerald Green. Dries well. O. T.

PERMANENT WHITE, barium sulphate, permanent and used only in water color.

ZINC WHITE *, oxide of zinc, also known as Chinese White in water color. Known since latter part of the 18th century. Mixes with all colors. Is very permanent. Dries slowly but sometimes cracks. O. W. T.

YELLOWS

AUREOLIN *, nitrate of cobalt and potassium, introduced 1861 and very permanent. Causes decomposition if mixed with organic pigments such as indigo, carmine, etc. Semi-transparent. O. W.

CADMIUM *, sulphide of cadmium, produced in many shades from a very pale yellow (Daffodil,

[16]

Aurora) through golden and orange shades to a red preferred by some artists to vermilion. Light shades not as opaque as orange. Used since the early part of 1800. It is very permanent. Do not mix with lead or copper colors. O. W. T.

CHROME, lead chromates, produced since early 19th century in many shades from lemon through golden and orange to red. Light shades not as opaque as darker ones. Fairly permanent. Have tendency to brown on exposure to light. Less expensive than cadmium. O. W. T.

GAMBOGE, a gum resin. Fades exposed to light but color is partially restored in dark. Does not mix with some of the metallic pigments such as lead, copper and iron colors. Is used in mixtures with Prussian Blue to produce Hooker's Greens. Very transparent. O. W.

INDIAN YELLOW, a magnesium-calcium salt of euxanthic acid. Not very permanent. Generally imitated with Yellow Lake, q. v. O. W.

JAUNE BRILLIANT, is a mixed color consisting of cadmium yellow, vermilion and a white. Varied considerably in composition and therefore cannot be considered permanent. O.

KINGS YELLOW, a mixture of pale chrome yellow with zinc white in which case permanency depends on their characteristics. For a more permanent mixture we would substitute cadmium yellow. On old color lists this was the yellow sulphide of arsenic, a very dangerous compound which blackened readily. Now practically obsolete. O.

YELLOW LAKE, a yellow dye of varying composition precipitated on an alumina hydrate base. Very fugitive. O. W.

LEMON YELLOW, barium chromate, very weak and pale. This is the most permanent of the pale chromate colors: barium, strontium and zinc. O. W.

MARS YELLOWS *, are artificial ochres containing more of the iron hydroxides and therefore have greater tinting strength. These also come in browns and reds of both yellowish and bluish tinge depending on the duration of calcination. O.

NAPLES YELLOWS, sometimes a lead antimoniate but nowadays mostly mixtures of zinc white, cadmium yellow and light red which excels the lead compound in permanence. Other mixtures are not as permanent. Opaque. O. W.

OCHRES *, clay stained with ferric hydroxides. One of the oldest pigments known. Very permanent, but in oil, because of great absorption of this, darkens as oil yellows. There are many fancy names for various shades. The one most generally used is the Light. These pigments roasted, lose some of their water in chemical combination and change to reds known as Flesh Ochre, Venetian and Light Red and so on. O. W. T.

SIENNAS, are similar to ochres but more trans-

[18]

parent. See ochres for characteristics. Require much more oil than ochres therefore darken more. More transparent than ochres. O. W. T.

STRONTIAN, strontium chromate, very pale and very weak tinting strength. Has greater permanency than zinc chromates. O. W.

ZINC YELLOW, zinc chromate, a good pale yellow but having a tendency to turn muddy-green in oil. Semi-transparent. O. W.

GREENS

CHROME GREENS, are mixtures of lead chromate and ferric ferrocyanide, chrome yellow and Prussian Blue. They vary in shade from pale yellowish greens in which the chrome yellow predominates to the dark bluish greens in which the Prussian Blue is present in higher percentage. Cover well. Have great tinting strength. Permanence and compatibility dependent on their components, q. v. O. W. T.

OXIDE OF CHROMIUM, *transparent* *, hydrated chromic oxide, discovered 1834. Known also as Viridian and Vert Emeraude. Very permanent and the artist's most useful green. Transparent. Do not confuse with chrome greens which do not compare in permanency. O. W. T.

OXIDE OF CHROMIUM, *opaque**, chrome oxide, A dull olive green, very permanent and useful.

[19]

Also known as Permanent Green. Opaque. O. W. T.

SAP GREEN, either an extract of unripe buckthorn berries or synthetically produced from fugitive dye mixtures. Transparent. Not Permanent. W. O.

TERRE VERTE *, a green earth akin to the ochres but its color is due to ferric silicates rather than oxides. Semi-opaque and weak tinting strength but quite permanent and useful. O. W. T.

VERDIGRIS, copper acetate, poisonous. Very fugitive. Transparent. Known by the Romans. O.

VERT EMERAUDE *, same as oxide of chromium, *transparent*, q. v. O. W. T.

VIRIDIAN *, same as oxide of chromium, *transparent*, q. v. O. W. T.

BLUES

ANTWERP, a Prussian blue diluted with alumina hydrate. See Prussian Blue for chemical composition and character.

CERULEAN *, a cobalt-tin oxide, very useful and permanent. Semi-opaque. O. W. T.

CHINESE, same as Prussian Blue, q. v.

COBALT *, a cobalt-aluminum oxide introduced early in the 19th century, very permanent and beautiful. Semi-opaque. O. W. T.

INDIGO, derived from a plant found in India and

Java of the Indigofera species. Known since earliest times. It is not as permanent as a pigment as it is as a dye. Most of it is now made synthetically. Used principally in water color, in oil mostly imitated by mixtures. Transparent. O. W.

NEW BLUE, just a name for a shade of ultramarine blue, q. v.

PERMANENT BLUE, see New Blue.

PRUSSIAN BLUE *, ferric ferrocyanide, discovered in 1704. Transparent, great tinting strength and of good permanency. O. W. T.

ULTRAMARINE *, a complex compound consisting of soda, sulphur, carbon and clays. Similar to the blue prepared since the 12th century from the semi-precious stone lapis-lazuli. This color is semi-transparent of a rich, useful, permanent blue. O. W. T.

PURPLES

MAGENTA, usually a precipitate of rhodamine on an alumina hydrate base, transparent, very fugitive and entirely unfit for artist's work. O. W.

MAUVE, usually a precipitate of methyl violet on an alumina hydrate base, transparent, very fugitive and should not be used in permanent work. O. T. W.

PURPLE LAKE, sometimes applied to a shade of

[21]

carmine and at other times to alizarine mixtures. Permanence depends entirely upon the components used. Transparent. O. W.

COBALT VIOLET *, a cobalt phosphate, a very beautiful and only really permanent violet. Semiopaque. Discovered about the middle of 1800. O. W. T.

REDS

ALIZARINE CRIMSON *, alizarine precipitated on an alumina hydrate base, really a synthetic madder lake but more brilliant, permanent and transparent. O. W. T.

CARMINE, a dye extracted from the cochineal insect and precipitated on an alumina hydrate base, known since the conquest of Mexico, 1523. Quite fugitive and now displaced by Alizarine Crimson which is permanent, q. v. O. W. T.

CRIMSON LAKE, a name for a shade of carmine usually a weaker precipitate of that dye.

GERANIUM LAKE; sometimes a lake precipitated from eosine (discovered 1870's) in which case it is very fugitive; at other times made from other more permanent coal tar dyes and then quite light fast. Make an exposure test to be sure which you have. Transparent. O. W. T.

HARRISON RED, sometimes a para red, sometimes a toluidine to imitate Vermilion. Some are permanent, others are not or are prone to bleed. Is not as opaque as Vermilion. O. W.

INDIAN RED *, a ferric oxide, with a decided purplish cast. Known since earliest times. Usually a natural product, but also made synthetically and then known as Mars Red or Ferrite Red. Very permanent. Opaque. O. W. T.

LIGHT RED *, a ferric oxide, usually produced by roasting yellow ochre. Opaque. Permanent. Palest of the red oxides. O. W. T.

MADDER LAKE, a dye extracted from the madder root precipitated on an alumina hydrate base. It contains both Alizarine and Purpurin. The latter has a tendency to fade and brown therefore the alizarine lake produced synthetically from coal tar is far more permanent as the purpurin is not present. See Alizarine Crimson. O. W. T.

PINK MADDER, formerly a very reduced precipitate of Madder Lake, q. v., but now usually made from Alizarine, q. v. O. W.

ROSE MADDER *, usually a weak precipitate of alizarine, formerly of madder root dye. O. W.

SCARLET LAKE, formerly a mixture of vermilion and crimson lake which was not very permanent, but now more generally vermilion and alizarine which is perfectly safe to use. Opaque. O. W.

VENETIAN RED *, an iron color akin to light red but somewhat darker. Opaque. Permanent. O. W. T.

[23]

VERMILION *, the red sulphide of mercury, known in Roman times in the natural state and produced artificially since the 12th century. Permanent and opaque. Various shades are known as English, French, Chinese and Orange. Do not mix with lead or copper colors. O. W. T.

AMERICAN VERMILION, an orange mineral base stained with eosine. Fugitive. O. W.

BROWNS

ASPHALTUM, a mixture of hydrocarbons usually called mineral pitch. Decomposed by sunlight, never dries, bleeds. Transparent. Should not be used by artists. O.

BITUMEN, another name for asphaltum, q. v.

BONE BROWN, produced by insufficiently calcining bones till they acquire a brown hue. Presence of impurities causes fading. Not permanent. O. W.

BROWN OCHRE, has properties of ochres, q. v., but is darker, browner in shade. O. W.

BROWN PINK, prepared from a precipitate of quercitron bark, transparent, very fugitive. O. W.

BURNT SIENNA *, roasting raw sienna produces this rich, red brown. Quite translucent and permanent. O. W. T.

BURNT UMBER *, the calcined raw umber produces this permanent, translucent warm brown. O. W. T.

[24]

CALEDONIAN BROWN, akin to an umber but somewhat richer, mostly imitated by mixtures of sienna and umber. Permanent. O. W.

CASSEL EARTH, same as Van Dyke Brown, q. v.

COLOGNE EARTH, see Cassell Earth.

ITALIAN PINK, see Brown Pink. O. W.

UMBER RAW *, a natural clay colored with ferric and manganese oxides. A greener brown than the Burnt Umber. Semi-opaque. Very permanent. O. W. T.

SEPIA *, a blackish-brown fluid secreted by the gland of a species of Mediterranean cuttle fish. Used only as a water color. Fair permanence. (Imitated in oil by mixtures of Van Dyke Brown and Lamp Black.)

VAN DYKE BROWN: a peaty earth pigment which, because of its partially decayed vegetable matter, fades on exposure to light. Semi-transparent. Not Permanent. O. W. T.

BLACKS—GRAYS

BONE BLACK, made by calcining bones. An inferior type of Ivory Black with similar characteristics.

BLUE BLACK *, also known as charcoal black and vine black, is made by the destructive distillation of wine lees. Permanent. Bluish undertone. O. W.

IVORY BLACK *, made from calcined ivory chips,

[25]

horn etc. This black is brownish in tone and very intense and covers well. Permanent. Decolorizes organic pigments. Dries better than lamp black in oil. O. W. T.

LAMP BLACK *, practically pure carbon, produced by burning oils or natural gas in insufficient air. Bluer undertone than ivory black. Permanent. Dries very slowly in oil. O. W. T.

MISCELLANEOUS

MEGILP, is not a pigment but is usually sold in tubes. It is a painting medium made by dissolving gum mastic in boiled oil treated with lead compounds and therefore acts as a drier. The use of this medium leads to disastrous later results such as cracks and darkening. O.

SUGAR OF LEAD, acetate of lead ground in linseed and essentially used as a drier. It is very quickly affected by sulphur and copper colors. Avoid its use. O.

GRAY TINT, a mixed color made of any of the blacks and whites. Supposed to be absolutely neutral in shade. It is a superfluous color. O.

PAYNE'S GRAY, a mixed color of a black, a crimson and a blue of the Prussian type. Of little use and questionable permanency. O. W.

CHAPTER III

CANVAS AND OTHER PAINTING GROUNDS

The choice of the painting surface is of greatest importance for future permanence and of direct influence on your technic. For oil paintings, canvas made of linen or cotton but preferably of the former prepared with a proper priming is used. The priming should be made of zinc white and chalk held together with a suitable binder and should be slightly absorbent to insure a thorough knit between pigment and ground. A white colored ground gives brightness to even the most opaque pigment and therefore should be given preference. On the other hand a slight cream tint or a pale gray are sometimes useful in giving a characteristic tonal quality to a picture. There is no doubt but that a harmony of colors is more easily reached on a tinted ground than on a pure dead white. The coarser grained canvases lend themselves to a free, open, impasto treatment, while detail in smoother finish is best executed on a finely woven canvas.

Water color painting in the English manner, that is, working only with transparent washes, must be executed on a white paper. Here again a rough surface has its advantages for freer handling—a smoother surface for detail. No white is used in the transparent method but all high lights are the white paper. All lightening of tints is produced simply by pale washes. This emphasizes the importance of the absolute whiteness of the paper, and naturally that made from only the best linen rags will remain whitest. The French method demands white pigment mixed freely with all the colors giving them an opaque quality. This method is called Gouasche. Here, as in oil color, a white ground brightens all colors but certain subjects or pleasing technical effects can be obtained on tinted papers.

Tempera is an opaque color by virtue of the character of its vehicle. Its execution can be carried out on canvas which should be slightly more absorbent than that used for oil colors. Water color paper, either white or tinted, can be used as well as any illustration board or cardboard panel. If the surface is greasy as sometimes oil color canvas is, or if the surface is not sufficiently absorbent, the surface should be scumbled with egg tempera medium to insure adhesion.

In oil painting the color as it is expressed from the tube is of satisfactory consistency for palette knife painting; for use with the brush the consistency must be slightly thinner. The diluent to use is important for too much oil added to the color will cause excessive yellowing. On the other hand, too much turpentine deadens the natural surface luster of the color. A good painting medium to use would be one part of damar varnish, one part of rectified turpentine and one part of refined linseed oil. Except where necessity demands it no driers should be used. A drop or two added to your palette cupful of medium just described will be sufficient.

Water color requires no special medium but a careful artist will use distilled water. The ordinary drinking water of some localities contains large amounts of mineral solubles which may affect some of the delicate pigments.

Tempera color can be painted with water alone as diluent if applied to a paper or cardboard surface. If the surface is oily or, on the other hand, hard and non-absorbent, a painting medium of one part egg tempera medium and one part of the water can be used for mixing the colors.

All paintings can and should be varnished as this forms a protective coating against atmospheric gases, and, if the right varnish is used, any dirt collected on the surface can be removed and the picture revarnished. This latter process is only practical with oil paintings, however, as on these the varnish lies as a separate coating on top of the paint film, whereas in water color and tempera, which are more or less absorbent, the varnish penetrates.

The varnish best suited for oil and tempera is damar. It does not yellow with age and can be removed with solvents which will not affect the oil paint film. Most of the water color varnishes are weak shellac solutions. All varnishes are best applied in a very thin film with a soft brush in a warm room on a dry day.

Retouching varnish is used only in connection with oil painting. It is usually a copal varnish very much diluted with very volatile rectified petroleum spirits and a little of an oleo resin added which acts as a softener on the paint film. When you work on an oil painting several days in succession parts will remain glossy, others will sink in flat. This throws values out. To continue, therefore, it is necessary to blow a mist of retouching varnish over the "sunk in" parts to bring them up. Just moisten the surface; do not drench it.

CHAPTER IV
COLOR THEORY AND STUDY

There are many systems of color study. Some are based on three colors—red, yellow and blue. Others on six colors, using crimson, a bluish red; a red like vermilion, which can be called a yellow red; and then green, violet, blue and yellow. There are still others using eight and twelve colors. Some distinguish between full bodied saturated colors and their hues which are either darkened by graying them or lightened by adding white. None of these gets away from the simple facts, however, that yellow and blue give green; blue and red, purple; and red and yellow, orange. The great majority of these systems are based on the physical theory of light which bears little if any relation to that of pigments.

It may be well for general information to give a short sketch of the theory of color based on the study of a ray of light broken into its component parts by the prism. The resulting color band, called the spectrum, shows the following colors merging by imperceptible gradation one into the other: red, orange, yellow, green, blue and violet. This band of colored lights impressed again on a prism reunite to form white light again. The physical difference between light and pigment, however, produces in a mixture of pigments representing the spectrum nothing but a dark neutral gray.

Newton and Helmholtz were the two great physicists who pioneered in the study of these light phenomena.

The presence therefore of light is the presence of color; the absence of all light—the absence of all color. If we view an object we see it by the light cast upon it reflected back to the retina of our eye. If the object is white all colors are reflected and the object appears white to us. If it is black all colors are absorbed and the object appears black to us. If it appears yellow then its surface has absorbed all but the yellow rays of the white light falling upon it and the yellow rays reflected to our eyes gives us the sensation of a yellow object.

As children we all have been taught the simple three color primary system—red, yellow and blue. We also learned that mixing these in pairs we produced green, orange and purple which are called secondaries. Reference to the first color plate will show the three color primary units. The second plate shows how the mixture of the blue and yellow produce green, the yellow and red an orange and the red and blue a purple.

Interesting to note is the overlapping of the blue and yellow triangles which have been graded from full color intensity to a mere tint so that the

[32]

PLATE I

PRIMARY COLORS

The upper three large squares show the elementary three unit primary system which forms the basis for many color theories. The lower set of six smaller squares represents the six unit primary. The colors in pigments for the latter, would be: Alizarine Crimson for the crimson, Vermilion for the red, Pale Cadmium Yellow for the yellow, a mixture of Verte Emeraude and Pale Cadmium Yellow for the green, Cobalt for the blue and Cobalt Violet for the violet. Zinc White added to this range of colors would give a very workable, simple, permanent palette.

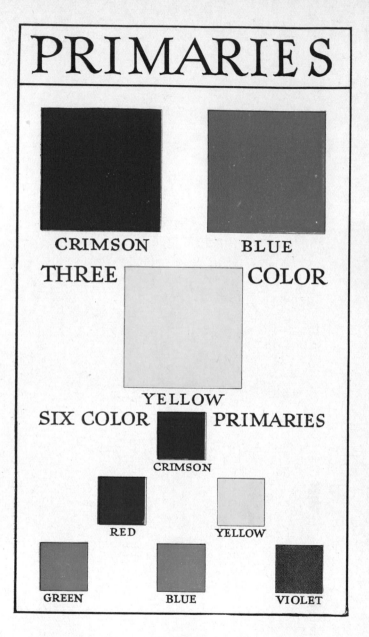

PRIMARIES

CRIMSON

BLUE

THREE

COLOR

YELLOW

SIX COLOR

PRIMARIES

CRIMSON

RED

YELLOW

GREEN

BLUE

VIOLET

PLATE I

SECONDARIES

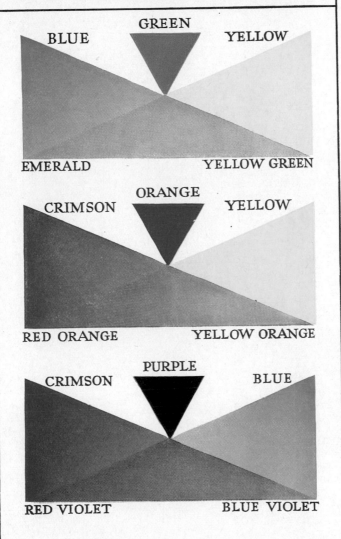

BLUE GREEN YELLOW

EMERALD YELLOW GREEN

CRIMSON ORANGE YELLOW

RED ORANGE YELLOW ORANGE

CRIMSON PURPLE BLUE

RED VIOLET BLUE VIOLET

PLATE II

PLATE II

SECONDARY COLORS

The mixture of any pair of primaries of the simple three color primary produces three new colors which are called secondaries. The diagrams illustrating this further show how the different proportions of the integrals give cool and warm greens and violets; the former showing an excess of blue, the latter a preponderance of yellow or red.

PLATE III

COMPLEMENTS

The mixture of a secondary with the primary not used in its mixture produces a neutral gray tone. When two colors mixed together produce a neutral gray they are said to be complementary to each other. A full realization of this attribute of color is important in painting in a two fold way. The artist who paints tonal pictures in a rather sombre key uses mostly neutralized colors. On the other hand for the painter in high key whose tones must be kept clean, clear—not muddy—the thorough knowledge of complements helps him avoid any neutralizing mixtures.

COMPLEMENTS

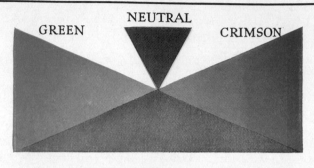

GREEN   NEUTRAL   CRIMSON

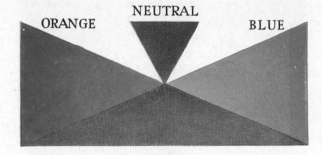

ORANGE   NEUTRAL   BLUE

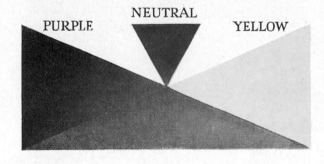

PURPLE   NEUTRAL   YELLOW

PLATE III

VALUES

| | 1 | 2 | 3 | 4 | 5 | 6 | 7 | 8 | 9 | 10 | |

N ... N

Y ... Y

G ... G

B ... B

V ... V

C ... C

R ... R

PLATE IV

PLATE IV

VALUES

Values are measurements of light and dark. White represents our highest light and black the deepest dark. We can tint color from its deepest saturation to its palest tint and consider this likewise a value measurement scale. Combined with this gradation of color we can superimpose the black and white value scale forming a series of grayed colors. These are valuable for comparison when painting in determining coolness or warmth of a tone. They also show the effect of reduced lighting, quasi addition of black, with intensified saturation of color.

full color of one primary is modified by just a tint of the other. It shows simply how color mixtures are made to the desired nuance by careful manipulation of the proportions of the components. Thus, the red and yellow in various mixture produce the *red orange* which is full saturated red with but a tint of yellow in it; or on the other hand the *yellow orange* in which the primaries predominate in inverse order.

On the page showing the simple three color primary system we have also shown the units comprising the six color system. This set of colors represented in pigments by Alizarine Crimson for the crimson, Vermilion for the red, pale Cadmium Yellow for the yellow, a mixture of pale Cadmium Yellow and Verte Emeraude for the green, Cobalt for the blue and Cobalt Violet for the violet would give with Zinc White an excellent simplified, permanent palette.

What then are the complementary colors? If we mix one of the secondaries with the primary which was left out in its mixture we get a neutral gray tone. In short then any two colors which if mixed together complete a neutral gray mixture can be called complements. For instance, purple is the secondary produced by the mixture of red and blue, leaving yellow to be used as the neutralizing agent. There are not only the three sets of complementary colors shown in the chart, but there is a complement for each color tone in one half of the overlapping triangles to be found in the other half. Naturally if one of the secondary tones is redder, as in the case of red orange, then its complementary must be weaker in that color. Blue is the complement of orange, but for red orange it must have less red and more yellow, which makes the complement for red orange a green blue.

In the diagrams to represent the complementaries visually we have the full value mixture to produce the neutral. We also have that overlapping of the secondary and primary colored triangles to show how different proportions of the integral colors produce an array of different colors again. Reference to older books on colors give these names such as citrine, russet and olive which as color names are hardly ever used today. As a fact the colors produced by these intermixtures cannot be as easily named as those produced by various proportions of the primaries in making the secondaries. The more complex the color mixture the less universally understood is the name applied to it.

Do not be satisfied to refer to these charts as you read—make them yourself on a large scale. The base of the overlapping triangles should be no less than ten inches long. Water colors, or even better, colored inks or water soluble dyes, should

[34]

be used for the color washes as these by super-imposition and their transparency produce the intermixtures you desire. To see more readily the demarcation of the various mixtures as the proportion of each primary or complement changes we would suggest dividing the ten inch base into inches and at each inch to erect a perpendicular, so that you have a series of bands. Then, instead of putting your wash on as a continuously grading full strength color to tint, color the full width of each strip with one tint of the gradation from full saturation of color to lightest tint. In water color you can use Yellow Lake for the yellow; Geranium Lake for the crimson, and Prussian Blue mixed with a little Cobalt for the blue. The dyes would be Ink Yellow, Eosine and Patent Blue or Alphazurine.

The page headed "values" gives you a scale of neutral tones which are valuable for reference when working in charcoal, black and white wash, pen and ink or pencil. The white of your paper would always be your highlight. Value number ten would be the general light illumination while number four would represent the shadow tone. Just as the general light illumination has its highlights, so the shadow tone has its highlights, more commonly called reflected light. This would have a value about like number seven. Accents would be represented by number one and real important

[35]

darks only should have a touch of absolute black.

Values then are gradations of light and dark, and taking the units of the six color primary and grading each of these from full color strength to lightest tint and super-imposing over this the neutral value scale we have a very interesting series of charts that serve as an aid to color perception.

The important part is to learn to see colors and then to learn by actual experience which pigments or which intermixture of pigments will represent the color seen.

We must often go to extremes to bring out by contrast rather than by actual representation the color effect we are striving for.

In the first place every object having mass will present its form by a contrast of light and dark in a pencil drawing. In a painting we must add to this cool and warm tones in contrast to bring the rotundity out. This again is affected by the source of the light whether this is cool or warm.

Objects in bright sunlight have their light side warm, their shadows cool. Objects in the studio or in shaded places receiving the cool reflected light of the blue sky will have warm shadows.

Modifying these simple possibilities are the reflected lights given off by objects standing close by.

Objects near us are seen in full intensity, full

saturation of colors. Strong contrasts appear between light and shade.

Objects in middle distance have their color saturation diminished by the haze of atmosphere between them and the eye. The contrast of light and shade is diminished.

Objects in the background and distance become but a pattern. The gamut of colors is blended into a fine tone with practically no distinction between light and shadow.

The effects of light and shadow, foreground and distances are brought about best by broken color.

If you are painting a distant hillside covered with green fields you cannot mix a green with some blue and white stirring it up thoroughly on the palette in perfect intermixture and get anything but a house paint tint. You mix all the vibration out of the color. If you set your hillside tone in green as a fresh green on the canvas and modify it there by dragging a light blue mixed with a little white over and through it you immediately simulate that vibration of atmosphere which makes that tone live.

The same principle is applicable to the middle distance and to the foreground. If you wish to represent an orange tone in the foreground a thoroughly mixed combination of red and yellow will be as lifeless and uninteresting as a painted table top. Lay in your red and drag yellow through it and you have an orange color glowing with life. You must not work for a flat cold representation but get the impression of a color.

A technic going still further in vibrant color is the pointillistic method. In this no colors are mixed but tones are built up of a stipple of pure, brilliant color.

It is recommended that the student make an earnest, systematic study of color mixtures, for even though certain mixtures will be given where definite instruction is outlined for landscape, still life, portraiture and figure painting, these mixtures are for unmodified conditions.

Sit down and take a blue, cobalt for instance, and have some white on your palette. Now mix this blue with alizarine crimson in three different proportions. One in which the proportion of blue is two parts to one of red; the second equal parts and the third consisting of two parts of red to one of blue. Grade part of each of these mixtures with white to the palest tint. It would be well to set a spot of each mixture on a canvas square as also to show the gradation with white. Note in pencil the pigments used.

Now try the same system of mixture with all other reds you have available, viz: Geranium, Vermilions, Earth Reds, such as Venetian, Light and Indian and so on.

Some of these mixtures will give deep purples

[38]

for accents or tinted with white, useful for flower tones. Others will be grayed lavenders such as are found in the fleecy clouds against a sunset sky or ideal representations for the heavily laden rain clouds.

Go through your whole palette and then try three color mixtures. This training will give you the ability to view a tone and analyze it in terms of pigments to use at a glance.

This color mixing practice is the only way to become acquainted with the mixing possibilities of the various colors. It is impossible, as has so often been done, to say that a cloud or stone or apple is represented by a mixture of so many parts of this with so many of that. Each color manufacturer's standards vary from the next not only in shade but also in strength. The only way to learn is to do it and then do it again.

CHAPTER V

LANDSCAPE PAINTING

Before you are ready to go out sketching take a piece of stiff black cardboard about three by four and one quarter inches and cut an oblong opening in the center about two by two and three quarter inches. This will give you an opening proportioned according to the laws of dynamic symmetry. This simple device is called a view finder and will be of inestimable value for determining the composition of the picture you choose to paint. Its use is not limited to landscape but can be used to advantage for all types of work.

After you have picked out your subject set up your easel and adjust the canvas or panel on it. Now set your palette with a simple assortment of colors beginning with zinc white at the right. The balance of the colors should follow to the left in the order named, viz: Pale Cadmium, Medium Cadmium and Orange Cadmium, Yellow Ochre, Raw Sienna, Opaque of Chromium, Verte Emeraude, Cerulean Blue, Cobalt Blue, Ultramarine, Prussian Blue, Cobalt Violet, Alizarine Crimson, Vermilion, Light Red, Burnt Sienna, Raw Umber and Black. One palette cup is filled with turpentine; the other with the painting medium.

Look at your subject through the view finder

and with a piece of charcoal indicate your composition on the canvas in large forms. Work with the lightest possible pressure. When you have blocked in the composition fairly well take one of the round bristle brushes and dip it into the turpentine and with this dilute some of the cobalt blue so that it is like a water color wash. With this carry out your drawing in charcoal in more detail. If you are a strong draughtsman you might draw direct with the brush which is recommended as soft charcoal is liable to dirty delicate tones. When this is done scumble some thinned color (diluted with turpentine) over the various areas approximating the local color of each area. This will give you a general tone to work with. And, as it should indicate in a rough way the large divisions of light and dark, gives something to go by to determine values.

Remember what was previously said about broken color and proceed with full color sparingly diluted with the painting medium if necessary. It is good to keep a rag, in the hand holding the palette and brushes, to be used for cleaning the surplus color off the brushes before you dip them into the turpentine for rinsing and cleaning. Try to keep your brushes in good order using some for light tones only and others for the dark tones.

Do not work up one portion of the picture in full detail and finish but try to pull all parts along

[41]

together at an even rate. The former method kills breadth and gives the picture a chopped up appearance; the latter creates unity and gives the picture balance.

Let me indicate in a general way how to arrive at some of the characteristic tones.

SKIES. A sky on a clear day is a strong blue overhead and tones down through greens to a lavender as it approaches the horizon. You have laid in your local color as Cobalt mixed with some White. Now take some Cobalt and drag it through the upper portions adding as you go down toward the horizon a little Verte Emeraude and White. As you proceed further add a minute quantity of Alizarine and more White.

CLOUDS. Sunlit clouds are always fascinating and interesting. Your local color should be white with a touch of pale yellow in it. The warm tone should then be segregated to the edges by building up the cold highlight on the cloud to nearly pure white. As you proceed to the lower parts of the cloud the tones are warmed with a medium yellow; deepened still further on with a touch of Alizarine which then tones to lavenders by the introduction of Cobalt Blue or even Verte Emeraude. The edges of the cloud are then toned into the background by breaking the warm color with a little pale crimson over into the blue.

TREES. Each species of tree has its own color

[42]

character ranging from the deep bluish green of the oak to the pale yellowish green of the birches. Your local color of the tree is separated into the warm tones where the sunlight floods it and into the cool tones of the shadow. Model the color of the tree now by working up to a cool highlight where necessary. If you are painting an oak the portion in the light should be made up of Verte Emeraude, Medium Yellow and a little Ochre; the shadowed portions of the same mixture cooled with Ultramarine. The deep accents of shadow can be either pure Ultramarine Blue or this mixed with a touch of Alizarine. For birches the local color of the light portion is mixed of pale yellow and Verte Emeraude; the cool portion the same base cooled with Cobalt or Cerulean Blue and a bit of White.

TREE TRUNKS. The oak trunk can be painted with Raw Umber, Burnt Sienna and Ochre in varying proportions according to the shade, and then modeled with Burnt Sienna and Ultramarine in the dark parts or to indicate the furrowed bark. Highlights are gotten with grays and lavenders. The former can be mixed by neutralizing three colors, red, yellow and blue, and adding white. The latter can be mixed from the grays by small excesses of red and one of the blues. The values in each instance are made by the addition of white. Spots of sunlight can be simulated by breaking

[43]

your light colored side with orange and vermilion mixed with white. Very deep accents such as knot holes or decay can be given resonance with an Alizarine-Prussian Blue mixture. The silvery tones of the birch trunks are brought about through lavenders and grays, which mixtures have already been discussed; the highlights in pure White tinged here and there faintly with Yellow Ochre. The markings of the bark can be touches of pure Ochre with accents of Umber. A spot of sunlight on the white trunks will throw the general light tone more to the bluish-lavender to bring out by contrast its coolness, compared with the warm sunlight. These sun-spots are tinged from this bluish-lavender shadow outside with quite a strong lavender, toning to crimson to pure pale yellow with a thick daub of white for the glare.

Now remember that as the trees recede into the background the contrast between light and shadow diminishes; the color is less intense. A bluish haze gathers strength making the light sides cool greens and the shadows become warm with gleamings of lavenders.

FIELDS. The prospect of a checkerboard of fields, some pale blue-green filled with corn, others yellow-green filled with sprouting young plants; again others gray-green which are hayfields just cut down and still others warm browns which have

[44]

just been tilled—such a prospect fascinates the artist and charms the beholder of the picture. Pale yellow and Verte Emeraude is the base color for the greens. A touch of White and Cerulean Blue gives you blue-greens and emerald greens. A medium yellow or even orange added gives you warm greens. The base alone produces the brilliant yellow-green of a freshly sprouted acre. Yellow Ochre, White and in some instances Burnt Sienna, in others Vermilion or still others Alizarine gives you the sunlit ploughed field. If the sun has dried the turned over ground the color is light; if it is freshly turned, Umber and Alizarine added gives the deep, damp richness of the soil.

SHRUBBERY—ROADS. The former of these is handled much in the same manner as trees and the latter like the tilled fields.

HOUSES. The red painted barn of New England and the gleaming white of colonial houses with their weather-beaten blue-green shutters add notes of living interest. The barns in actuality are painted with one of the red oxide colors and we will find that Light Red for the light and Indian Red for the shadowed portions are about right, but naturally these must be grayed to reproduce the weather-beaten effect. Perhaps a tree casts shadows on the barn—add some blue to your color, like a Cobalt. For accents such as cracks between the boards use a stronger blue like Prussian with your red earth color. The white house has tones similar to the white bark of the birch. The green shutters are Verte Emeraude, Cobalt, White and a touch each of pale Yellow and Ochre to show the discoloration of time.

BROOKS—LAKES. The ripple of a brook is attractive to some while others prefer the calm of a mirror-like lake or dam with its reflections. The stones of the brooks are usually grays and lavenders with shadings to pale Ochre where •they are exposed to the air and covered with algæ. Where the water level rises and falls a rich green moss grows. Under water the stones are slimy with mud browns and brown greens. The saturated, rich greens of moss are mixed from Verte Emeraude and medium Yellow. The darker shades are produced by adding Prussian Blue. The mud browns are Umber and Ochre toned sometimes with a touch of Burnt Sienna or Alizarine, other times with deep greens. The water as such is colorless and running over the stones you see through it these dark browns and brown-greens. The play of ripples over the surface reflects the colors of foliage, tree trunks and sky. Here and there as it falls sharp over or between two stones a white highlight appears.

The placid mill pond is colored by the color of the bottom, the colored objects on its surrounding banks and the sky overhead. A reflection is never as intense as the object reflected. There is just a tone, a very fine, distinctive difference in value. The more accurately this is reproduced the finer is the ability of the artist to appreciate delicate nuances.

When painting with water colors your choice of colors is the same. Your method of procedure is different, however, in that you must proceed by carefully laid washes one over the other to get your mixtures, remembering always that your white paper is the white with which you mix pale tints. As the work progresses you get stronger and stronger in color and in accent. Often the best effects are produced by blending a color into one which is wet letting accidental mixtures and mottlings of color play their part. Your body or opaque colors, if any are used, should be mainly in the foreground.

With tempera one can proceed as with oil colors, or just as with water color. Another technique calls for a combination of both methods. In either case the flat drying color, lean in vehicle, will give beautiful pastel-like tones.

CHAPTER VI

STILL LIFE AND FLOWERS

On rainy days the artist turns to either composing pictures from the sketches made outdoors or freshens his color study by the contrast of a still life study. There are many utensils, vases and odds and ends in every one's possession even if they are of most lowly origin which can be grouped to form an interesting study in composition, color and color values. Often the most accidentally placed objects stacked into a corner or left on a table form the most interesting subjects.

A combination of whites of different textures— tablecloth, china, books and silver—would form a very difficult study in high-key. A darkened corner with old dusty dark colored vases, unpolished copper kettle and withered leaves would be a subject for low-key study.

The composition can be viewed now and then through the view finder during the arranging process until an interesting placement of each object is accomplished.

The palette for a low-key picture is different from one for a high key. Let me present them to you for comparison.

HIGH-KEY PALETTE: White, Pale Yellow, Orange, Yellow Ochre, Verte Emeraude,

[48]

Prussian Blue, Ultramarine Blue, Cobalt Blue, Cerulean Blue, Alizarine Crimson, Vermilion and Light Red.

LOW-KEY PALETTE: White, Pale Yellow, Medium Yellow, Orange, Yellow Ochre, Raw Sienna, Terre Verte, Opaque Oxide of Chromium, Verte Emeraude, Prussian Blue, Ultramarine Blue, Cobalt Blue, Alizarine Crimson, Vermilion, Indian Red, Burnt Sienna, Raw Umber and Black.

In the painting of a group of white objects you will notice that they are not just solid white paint but that each one is made up of a myriad of pale colored tones reflected from the objects about them or from the source of light. Again there is that play of cold and warm tones which added to the light and shadow brings out the solidity of the object and separates it from the other objects and background. Then, the highlights on the white cloth are soft while on porcelain or metal they stand out crisp.

The introduction of some fruit forms a contrasting note of color and helps bring out the charm of the various white textures.

The tones of these various whites are produced by reductions to the same value of the various colors such as Verte Emeraude, Prussian Blue, Ultramarine and Cobalt with white for the cool tones. The Yellows, Orange, Ochre, Alizarine

Crimson, Vermilion and Light Red reduced similarly with white produce the warm tones. In the shadows these can be grayed by neutralizing them with their complementaries.

The fruit can be handled as follows: bananas are painted with pale yellow mixed with some white for the plane turned toward the light. The next adjoining plane can have a touch of Ochre mixed in and the darker ones a little warm green. The points shade to an emerald green (Verte Emeraude, Pale Yellow, Cerulean Blue and White) with the dark spot a touch of Alizarine Crimson and Ultramarine, or perhaps a warm brown where it has been pulled from the stem.

An apple is either a bluish green shading to yellowish green where it has ripened, or it may be green with markings of red. The mixtures for the greens are evident from the previous color mixtures noted in the chapter on landscape. The red markings start with a mixture of the pale Yellow with Alizarine Crimson; the latter pigment coming in excess as you move toward the shadow. For the deepest shadow tones in this red a bit of Ultramarine can be introduced.

Pears are yellow-green and russet. The russet tone should be easy for you if you have tried out the mixing studies outlined in a previous chapter. Green and orange which can be in some cases straight orange color or Yellow Ochre and Vermilion or Yellow Ochre and Alizarine produce the russet tone.

In a low-key painting the colors must be full bodied and saturated. This means we must economize in the use of White. Warm tones are lightened with various Yellows. Cool tones are lightened with Cobalt or Cerulean Blue. White is added only when either of these colors as intermixtures becomes too prominent.

Do not go to extremes in the use of lights and accents but leave these touches for the last bit of painting. If you shoot your highest light and deepest dark right at the beginning you will have nothing left to give your painting snap. Your dark accents are best made of Prussian Blue and Alizarine Crimson which as a dark accent is much more effective than black.

Many still life subjects contain flowers. In the painting of these it is very important to watch your brush strokes. These should always be laid around and over the form to help simulate the planes of the surface. The careful detailing of the flower and its minute components is never as effective as trying in a simple manner to suggest these details. A flower worked out in hard detail presents a waxy, artificial appearance. A flower with all detail, but that suggested, gives the beholder that ethereal beauty of the flower—that evanescent charm.

For flowers like the pansy we need pure yellows, deep velvety purples (Ultramarine and Prussian Blue with Alizarine).

On the other hand roses and sweet peas require delicate pinks and lavenders or shadings of these. The pinks are made of either Alizarine and White for the cool pinks or Vermilion and White for the warm pinks. A blue like Cobalt added to the former gives lavenders of purest shades. On the other hand a Yellow Ochre and a touch of pale Yellow with Alizarine Crimson and White produces salmon pink shades. Other variations of pink can be produced by the mixture of the basic Alizarine Crimson-Vermilion pinks mentioned at the beginning of this paragraph.

Yellow Chrysanthemums have their high lights made of pale Yellow and White, the shadow side is deepened with Yellow Ochre with a shimmering of green toward the centers. The white ones present a problem of a myriad of high-keyed tones such as were found in painting the high-keyed still life whites.

Geraniums of a deep red and other similar colored flowers such as roses and dahlias have their lights painted of Vermilion and Alizarine Crimson mixtures with pure Alizarine Crimson for the shadow side with accents of this crimson mixed with Ultramarine.

CHAPTER VII

PORTRAITS AND FIGURES

Most every artist tries to attain what is considered the highest goal in art: portrait painting. Not merely good drawing, but a sense of caricature is necessary to grasp those salient lines of the sitter's features which when recorded and accented produce that something which is character and likeness. The color is clothing for the drawing which must fit so that though present, the beholder is not conscious of it but sees it only as heightening the presentation of the type painted.

The sitter for a portrait should not be posed or else the finished picture will look like a manikin. Talk with your subject until at ease, study facial characteristics but do not overlook the attitude of the body accompanying these. When the sitter has at last settled into a comfortable pose, one which can be maintained or retaken after rest periods, move about with your view finder in your hand studying the composition from various angles. When you have finally found the most satisfactory one move your easel to that point of view.

Your drawing should be carefully made in charcoal and then fixed by blowing a good fixatif over it sparingly with an atomizer. Do not flood the surface, for fixatifs are shellac solutions which do

[53]

not present a good surface for oil paint and further act as a filler taking away that vital absorbency of the ground.

Your palette for portrait work should be simple: White, pale Yellow, medium Yellow, Orange, Yellow Ochre, Opaque Oxide of Chromium, Verte Emeraude, Terre Verte, Ultramarine, Prussian Blue, Cobalt, Cobalt Violet, Alizarine Crimson, Vermilion, Light Red and Raw Umber.

When you are ready to paint go at it feverish, inspired. Try to get the large form of the head during the first hour of the sitting. Details such as careful drawing of the ears, eyes and mouth should not be touched. Try to get a likeness in the large forms first. When I said, "details of ears, eyes and mouth" I did not wish to convey the impression that they are details but rather that they are elements which produce a disturbing effect by drawing the artist's attention away from the likeness of the big forms. When you are satisfied with the latter, set in the eyes and other details and you will be surprised how quickly the whole head comes to life-like similarity.

Cool flesh tones are made of pale Yellow, Alizarine and White; warm ones of Yellow Ochre, Vermilion and White. The former are shaded with blues for cool and Terre Verte for warm modelling touches; these can be deepened with Light Red or Umber to give accents. Terre Verte will be found a valuable color to break both cool and warm tones to give those pearly variations so characteristic of skin texture with its play of veins underneath.

Sometimes a full red touch in the corner of the eye, nose or ear will lend a flesh tone to all surrounding tones.

Keep all your shadows transparent. Nothing spoils a portrait so much as heavy, opaque, muddy shadows.

The lips, in the highlight are Vermilion, toned down a bit with Alizarine Crimson. The shadows can be gotten with Alizarine, and the accents by mixing Umber with this.

The hair must receive very individual treatment for it varies so much in color. It must approximate with a mixture of many colors the hair of the subject. The highlights must be crisp on oily, glossy hair; and more diffused on dry hair.

In all portrait, as well as figure work the modelling of the features or dress is considerably aided by laying the brush strokes in conformity with the planes of the mass. Broken color is as effective in portrait and figure painting as in landscape or still life. The careful use of cool and warm tones in light and shadow adds to the modelling of the head.

The sitter's dress is sometimes carried out in broad masses and at other times in great detail.

[55]

The personality of some lies mainly in the features or in the carriage of the head on the body. On the other hand, an officer's uniform is interesting paintable material which adds to the picture. Fashion nowadays is so changeable that a woman's portrait of ten years ago looks rather grotesque to eyes of today if the dress has been literally rendered. On the other hand, military attire (as just mentioned), a judge's gown or for that matter a fanciful costume are not subject to fashion and remain fresh in interest always.

To give variation, or to prevent a face from being too strongly divided by light and shadow the artist uses a light colored reflecting screen background to cast a reflected light upon the shadow side of the head. Usually if the main source of light is cool the reflected one is warm. The effectiveness of a reverse of this lighting scheme is also good. In this type of representation your darkest shadows come at high points between the two light masses, as for instance the ridge of the nose.

A small illustration of the lighting of the eye here may suggest to you the careful observant way you should proceed to reason out the why and wherefore in effects of color. The eye ball is white normally, but due to strain or disease the network of minute blood vessels is distended making it reddish and yellowish. The iris is of various

·colors in different persons but in all it is semi-transparent. Light falling on this circular mass passes through it so that the section adjacent to the circumference furthest from the eye is lighter than where the light strikes it. The pupil is a dark looking spot due to the opening into and through the liquid content of the eye ball. It is the darkness of the iris at the point of lighting that forms such a wonderful contrast for the high-light.

Figure painting does not demand the portrait-like accuracy of the features, nor does it permit of sketchy treatment of the costume for in this type of work the figure becomes an integral part with foreground, background, accessories or other figures to form a pleasing design or composition. To give color instruction for this type of work would be nigh impossible because of the multi-tude of variations possible in texture, color, and lighting. If the student has gone through with his color mixing suggestions; has tried some of the hints in regard to landscape, still life and por-traiture, he will have a good fund of knowledge with which to embark on this genre.

CHAPTER VIII

RÉSUMÉ

This last chapter contains thoughts and suggestions which do not belong to any one of the chapters but are applicable as a whole to all of them. Added to these ideas are a few words of warning, also of encouragement.

Hokusai said when about ninety that could he live another hundred years he might be able to draw. Our own Edison remarked that genius is one per cent inspiration and ninety-nine per cent perspiration. From the one you can take that an artist, no matter what honors he may receive or how perfect he may become, must still remain the student. The other remark covers all those long-haired, cigarette-smoking, tea-sipping, deep-thinkers who have the popular conception of the artist veneered over them from head to foot but who just loathe work. Plenty of hard work, well directed by an active, studious mind make successes in art as in other endeavors.

Books on a subject such as this can no more teach you to paint than going through the movements of swimming on a couch will give you the ability to keep your body afloat on water. Actual doing and then *more actual doing* along the line of the suggestions made is the thing. That is the point, a book like this is a guide—it can but point the way.

You will notice that none of the color mixtures say: to produce Stone Brown use so many parts of this and so many of that. It would be more than useless to do that, for each color manufacturer has his own standards as regards the shade of colors and the strength of pigments used for these. A "so many part" mixture could vary not only by the number of different color manufacturers but also by the number of people making any of those mixtures.

The lure of the modernities of art movements has called many a good carpenter from his saw in the belief that he could daub up a rag stretched on four pieces of wood and label it with an abstruse title. Look carefully at those artists who really are names in cubism or subjectivism and turn back to their early training and work. They knew how to draw. They knew how to paint. They have essenced that knowledge now to express a definite line of reasoning. In modern art as in all art that with the strongest foundation and equipment will speak through the ages.

Do not hurry with your work but plod and experiment. You must ferret out all manner and means for obtaining a variety in color and technique to best express yourself. When once you have discovered, either intentionally or accidentally, a super-effective way of doing a certain thing do not repeat it in a hundred variations. You will only be a rubber stamp if you do. Aside from this, the world is full of unscrupulous copyists who may make their copy better than your original if you have not stored away that necessary experience to keep just a jump ahead of them.

If you are honest with your work and with yourself you need no critics to boost your wares—your inner self will tell you if you have really achieved something or just produced "another one of those ——."

Some students draw with ease, but compose or paint with difficulty. Others have facility in composition but labor with sweaty brow to get their drawing and color. That is natural with most of us. Take for example arithmetic. One will fly up and down a column of figures and get a correct answer but find division and multiplication hard. Another will relish the latter and detest the former. If you have some one phase come easy to you do not keep doing that over and over or else you will become one-sided. Stress those things you do not do so well till their command by your hand, eye and mind is up to par with your natural facilities. What good would a mathematician be if he could only add with ease and exactness? About as good as an artist who could only paint but not draw or compose!

[60]

Copying as study is good, but the copy you work from must be worthy of study.

There should be no such term as "commercial art." There is no reason why a man endowed with the power to portray things so that they attract buyers is any less an artist than the worker who hammers a piece of silver, designs a textile or plans an interior to become something sought for. Thanks to the vision of many large concerns some of our best talent has graced this field of art.

One hears and reads much about the "secret of the old masters" or remarks to the effect that had so and so been able to use the colors the old masters used then his work would not now be in the state of ruin it is. The only secret the old masters had was that they were good craftsmen and applied their colors according to the dictates of what experience had taught them. Their pigments were limited. Many of them were fugitive and others interacted with other colors just as do our pigments today. We are more fortunate and more unfortunate today. Fortunate because the control of chemical processes is so exact that we can obtain pigments in a much purer state. Unfortunate because many colors have been discovered which may find a use in other arts but which should never be found on the artist's palette. But, even with this fortunate advantage and a designation by interested color manufacturers as to what

[61]

pigments are fugitive there is something lacking—
and that is the technical knowledge of the crafts-
man. The old masters knew their material as they
knew their anatomy and perspective and that was
their secret of permanence.

A color like Verdigris, which Van Eyck used
extensively, is a dangerous pigment in conjunc-
tion with practically any other color. It is an un-
stable copper acetate which would readily break
up with either lead or sulphur colors or be darkened by atmospheric chemicals. It is still sold today but how many artists know of its danger?
Van Eyck carefully insulated this color from all
others and the air by means of balsam-varnishes,
before it was applied and after it had dried.

That is today's difficulty—convenience. Every-
thing is bought in tubes and bottles ready for use.
The young student wants to paint. He looks to
see what his neighbor has. He inquires of the clerk
behind the counter of the supply store. Both the
neighbor and clerk have no technical knowledge
with which to start him off right. Regrettably, it
must also be said that many of the artist-in-
structors cannot give a bit of *real* technical advice.
Every one concentrates on producing an effect—
but how, with what kind of material, makes no
difference to the ninety and nine out of the hundred. We must become craftsmen with absolute

[62]

control over our material and to do this we should know its structure, its uses, its limitations.

Color is either a thing by itself or an integral part in the consideration of beauty. There are many who have started out on the broad highway of art mounting lofty peaks only to find themselves obsessed with the color idea. One may fall by the way-side to study the chemistry of the color-giving pigment. The other may work out formulas by which color may be analyzed in measurements of its vibrations. The third applies his findings to the therapeutic value of color on mental balance. The subject of color is colored by many romances, many of which still are unlived and untold.